ABCs of Gratitude

Giving thanks
through the alphabet
for your blessings

Scripture taken from the HOLY BIBLE, NEW INTERNATIONAL VERSION. Copyright © 1973, 1978, 1984 International Bible Society. Used by permission of Zondervan Publishing House.

All inquiries should be addressed to:
Kimberley Payne
www.kimberleypayne.com

Table of Contents

Introduction

Pastor Tristin, the youth pastor at my church, shared in our small group meeting that he had to travel a long distance with a teenager. In order to make the drive more enjoyable they played a "game" of going through the alphabet and picking one thing for which they were grateful. Starting with the letter A, the pastor, then his travel companion, said something each was thankful for, and they did this back and forth until the letter Z.

Not only was it a memorable trip, but both men felt a sense of peace and joy through the process of proclaiming their gratitude.

I felt inspired by Pastor Tristin's story and that same day I created a Facebook group page called the *ABCs of Gratitude*. I challenged my Facebook friends to join the group and for the next 26 days we shared what we were thankful for, choosing words starting with the letter of the day.

What an encouragement! Just reading about the things for which my friends were thankful reminded me to be grateful as well. It sparked my imagination and gave me an inner sense of wonderment and joy.

The lifting of spirits through the process of proclaiming what one is thankful for has been well documented. I enjoyed the challenge so much that I decided to lift it from the space of Facebook and put it into book form.

To help stir your imagination, I've chosen one quote from the original Facebook challenge, along with a list of other things for which participants expressed gratitude to help stir your own thoughts about gratitude. The list is by no means exhaustive but only for fodder.

If you'd like to share your new ideas you are welcome to send me an email (kimberleypayne@nexicom.net) and I'll sign you up to join the Facebook group.

I pray you find deep joy and peace as you work through the 26 days of the ABCs of gratitude.

~ A ~

Authors, air, attitude, authority, advice, apples, appreciation, atonement, adoption, anticipation, all, aunts ...

"Awed by God's willingness to make something out of my life, and appreciate how He patiently waits for me to spiritually grow up. Acknowledging that without God my life has no meaning." Ramona Furst

~ B ~

Bible, babies, buds, books, blooms, buddies, blessings, benefits, breath of life, boys, bees and butterflies, birds, birthdays, bicycles, beauty, bananas and blueberries ...

"Beauty - I'm thankful for all of the beauty in nature that God provides. Simple little things, from a raindrop about to fall off of someone's face, to the clouds on a sunny day! Sometimes it's breathtaking." Andi Harris

~ C ~

Canada, children, cameras, courage, conviction, Christ, cars, comfort, creativity, chocolate, cats, chickens, charity, companionship, challenges, coffee, church, cartoons, clothes ...

"Being involved in Children's Ministry, I am thankful for children! They are all sent to us from heaven and they remind me of what God sees when He looks at us."
Joanita Nakimuli

~ D ~

Dads, daughters, days, dogs, deliverance, driving, doctors, devotion, dancing, democracy, diversity ...

"I am grateful for my Heavenly Dad. The Bible talks about us being able to call Him 'Abba,' which essentially translates as 'Daddy.' And that is also a unique and blessed relationship found in no other faiths." Kathy Birkett

~ E ~

Eternity, energy, evangelists, experiences, excitement, exuberance, education, eggs, exercise, everlasting life, eyes and ears, envelopes , evergreens, endurance, endorphins ...

"I am grateful for the equilibrium that comes with experience and age. Equilibrium as in balance, composure, stability and steadiness—not necessarily in our bodies and health, but in our minds and our spirits." Ruth Meyer

~ F ~

Friends, flowers, fiction, forgiveness, fun, family, freedom, faith, favour, fruit, fingers, feet, faithfulness, food ...

"Whether at a festivity or a funeral, I am thankful for feelings, that God has not made us emotionless, robotic. Really appreciate that we, like ice cream, come in a variety of flavours, and express our feelings, fabulous or forlorn, in a range of form or fashion." Sheila Steel

~ G ~

God, girlfriends, grace, gifts, goodness, growth, grandparents, guitars, giggles, gratitude, green, godly influences, generosity, gravy ...

"I am also thankful for the gathering of God's people on Sunday mornings."
Dawna Hawkshaw

~ H ~

Holy Spirit, house and home, health, happiness, holiness, heat, heaven, hymns, husband, hot chocolate, harmony, healing ...

"H is for Hesed, Hebrew for God's unfailing love." Judi Peers

~ I ~

Immanuel, innocence, internet, instructions, interests, ingenuity, innovative inventions ...

"Indebtedness - to my father, my mother and other military personnel who served and paid the ultimate sacrifice." Glynis Belec

~ J ~

Jesus, joy, justification, jazz music, justice, Jehovah Jireh, January, jubilee, jackets, jewels ...

"I am thankful for Jesus, my literal savior, without whom my life would not be the life I have today." Loretta Anne Potje-Bouillon

~ K ~

Kindle and Kobo, keyboard, knowledge, kindness, kudos,
kindred spirits, kingdom coming, kittens, knots ...

"I'm grateful for the King of Kings who
teaches us to be kind." Ruth Snyder

~ L ~

Lord Jesus Christ, literature, literacy, literary, livelihood, laughter, learning, love, licorice, lunch, lessons, library ...

"I give thanks for the Lord and the love and life He has given me." Jo-Anne Upton

~ M ~

Money, music, mom, mysteries, mercy, marvels ...

"M is for Music. Especially praise and worship music." Jan Cox

~ N ~

New beginnings, nieces and nephews, novels, notebooks, neighbours, nature, news ...

"I am grateful for the Navitity which brings me to worship the babe born to be our Lord and Savior. If we didn't have the Navitity we wouldn't have the Cross."
Ruth Sakstad

~ O ~

God's omnipotence, options and opportunities, oxygen, outer space, optimists and overcomers, outdoors, orange juice ...

"And orchids, orchards, olives, and orioles – the uniqueness and beauty of our Lord's creation and the opportunities to delight in them." Krysia Lear

~ P ~

Prayer, patience, pianos, peace, psalms and proverbs, pies,

purpose, pastors, provision, poetry, puzzles, presents, praise ...

"I am very grateful for my wonderful, anointed, and awesome pastors. I am grateful for my husband who is also a pastor." Ruth Ann Holloway-Adams

~ Q ~

Questions, quiet time, quilts, quality, Q-tips ...

"Q is qualm, not tolerating sin and falling into traps of the enemy." Dar Lilly

~ R ~

Redemption, relationships, resurrection, rollercoasters, rest, rejuvenation, restoration, revival, rain, rainbows, resilience, reading, raspberries, renewal, reading, relaxing, recliners ...

"I am thankful for the relationship we have with our heavenly Father. What an awesome gift! Relationship with the God of the universe! Wow!" L Shoshana Rhodes

~ S ~

Showers, Saviour, soap, Scrabble, snow, sound, salvation, security, singing, sacrifice, sleep, surprises, safety, sisters ...

"I'm grateful for salvation and security because of Christ's sacrifice." Patricia Elford

~ T ~

Testimonies, technology, teeth, today, thinkers, teachable spirit, triumph, tea, teenagers, teachers, tennis, tulips ...

"I'm thankful for testimonies that remind us of how God works in each of our lives."
Stephanie Nickel

~ U ~

Umbrellas, underwear, universities, unconditional love, u-turns, unity …

"I am grateful for those moments of unbridled joy!" Sally Meadows

~ V ~

Victory in Jesus, virtues, variety, vanilla flavouring, vision, virgin birth of our saviour, vitamins, vacations, violets, voting ...

"I am grateful for vision. Both in the natural world and in the glimpses of what God sees." Betty LePage

~ W ~

Wi-Fi, wind, words, weather, watermelons, warmth, water, waterfalls, whispers, wisdom, weekends, windows, wit, wonder, walks, work, wellness, wonder ...

"I am thankful for words of wisdom. I seek them from the Word of God every day." Krystal Kuehn

~ X ~

X-rays, "Xanadu" the classic song, xanthous (red-haired), Xerox
machines ...

*"Xylophone—This is symbolic. The church I
grew up in often had missionary speakers.
If they played a musical instrument, they
often brought that and provided "special
music" as we called it. I remember being
impressed with one speaker who set up
his xylophone and played it. So I'm letting
that stand for the strong missionary
grounding that I had in childhood."*
Audrey Dorsch

~ Y ~

Yahweh, Yeshua, yogourt, yellow, yuletide, years, yesterdays, yams, youth, yards ...

"I'm thankful for all my redeemed Yesterdays and for the untiring Zealous nature of my Father God!" Marlene VanderLaan

~ Z ~

Zoo, zinc, zest for life, zebras, zippers ...

"Zeal to live my life zealously,
unabashedly and always for Christ."
Ramona Furst

Concluding Thoughts

Many thanks to the contributors: Glynis Belec, Kathy Birkett, Peter Black, Jan Cox, Audrey Dorsch, Patricia Elford, Ramona Furst, Andi Harris, Dawna Hawkshaw, Ruth Ann Holloway-Adams, Krystal Kuehn, Krysia Lear, Betty LePage, Dar Lilly, Sally Meadows, Ruth Meyer, Joanita Nakimuli, Stephanie Nickel, Judi Peers, Loretta Anne Potje-Bouillon, L Shoshana Rhodes, Ruth Sakstad, Ruth Snyder, Sheila Steel, Jo-Anne Upton, and Marlene VanderLaan.

I'm especially grateful for the One who is "the Alpha and the Omega, the beginning and the end."

He is the A to the Z and the sum total of everything in between—the Living Eternal Word of God, who was with God in the beginning and even before time began, and who is God forever blessed.

I'm grateful that in Him I live and move and have my being. It is all of His mercy and grace.

~~~

Peter Black

Psalm 136

¹Give thanks to the LORD, for he is good.
His love endures forever.
²Give thanks to the God of gods.
His love endures forever.
³Give thanks to the Lord of lords:
His love endures forever.
⁴to him who alone does great wonders,
His love endures forever.
⁵who by his understanding made the heavens,
His love endures forever.
⁶who spread out the earth upon the waters,
His love endures forever.
⁷who made the great lights—
His love endures forever.
⁸the sun to govern the day,
His love endures forever.
⁹the moon and stars to govern the night;
His love endures forever.
¹⁰to him who struck down the firstborn of Egypt
His love endures forever.
¹¹and brought Israel out from among them
His love endures forever.
¹²with a mighty hand and outstretched arm;
His love endures forever.
¹³to him who divided the Red Sea[a] asunder
His love endures forever.
¹⁴and brought Israel through the midst of it,
His love endures forever.
¹⁵but swept Pharaoh and his army into the Red Sea;
His love endures forever.
¹⁶to him who led his people through the wilderness;
His love endures forever.
¹⁷to him who struck down great kings,
His love endures forever.
¹⁸and killed mighty kings—
His love endures forever.
¹⁹Sihon king of the Amorites
His love endures forever.
²⁰and Og king of Bashan—
His love endures forever.
²¹and gave their land as an inheritance,
His love endures forever.
²²an inheritance to his servant Israel.
His love endures forever.
²³He remembered us in our low estate
His love endures forever.
²⁴and freed us from our enemies.

His love endures forever.
[25] He gives food to every creature.
His love endures forever.
[26] Give thanks to the God of heaven.
His love endures forever.

***

About the Author

Kimberley Payne is a motivational speaker and author who writes on topics to encourage moms in fitness, family, and faith.

Through her work, Kimberley hopes to inspire mothers to live healthier lives that glorify God.

Your Free Gift

As a way of saying thank you for your purchase, I'm offering my devotional, <u>Where Family Meets Faith</u>. When you subscribe to my newsletter via email, you will get free access to download the ebook. You can download this free ebook by going to <u>www.kimberleypayne.com</u>

I am very grateful for reviews. If you liked this book, please take a moment to write a review on Amazon and Goodreads.

Made in the USA
Charleston, SC
05 March 2015